Contents

Introduction – Page 2
Before the Series – Page 3
First Test – Page 5
Individual Performances – Page 7
Second Test – Page 8
Series Records – Page 10
Third Test – Page 11
Commentary – Page 13
Fourth Test – Page 15
Catches – Page 17
Fifth Test – Page 18
Extras – Page 20
2006/7 Series – Page 21
Answers – Page 24

The Ashes 2005 Quiz Book

Introduction

The Ashes series played between England and Australia in 2005 is considered one of the great contests in the history of cricket. For many fans, the matches played between the two sides in 2005 will always be the peak of their lives as cricket supporters.

From the build up to the series all the way through to its stunning conclusion, this book provides an array of questions about the series, with details of every test match, the remarkable events and those individuals who created such incredible moments throughout that summer.

Before The Series – *Answers on page 24*

1) What was the score in the previous ashes series in Australia in 2002/3?

2) What was the winning margin in the T20 international game played between the two sides?

3) In the T20 game, at one stage Australia lost 7 wickets for 8 runs, which two England bowlers took those 7 wickets?

4) Which other national side competed with England and Australia in the tri-nations one day competition?

5) What was the result in the final of the 50 over tri-nations competition?

6) In the eighth match of the tri-nations series, Matthew Hayden was enraged after being hit by a throw from which England bowler?

7) Following the tri-nations final, England and Australia played a further three match one day series, what was the result?

8) Which future Ashes winning fast bowler made his England debut in the tri-nations tournament?

9) Which young Australian all-rounder was apparently scared by a ghost whilst staying at Lumley Castle before the one day international at Durham?

10) Ashley Giles missed the two match test series against Bangladesh, which spinner replaced him in the side?

11) Which player made his 100th, and final, test appearance for England in that series?

First Test – *Answers on page 26*

1) Which ground was the match played at?

2) Name the two line-ups

Australia	**England**
?	?
?	?
?	?
?	?
?	?
?	?
?	?
?	?
?	?
?	?
?	?

3) What was the result?

4) Who won the man of the match award?

5) Who bowled the first ball of the series?

6) Who took the first wicket in the series?

7) Which player had the highest individual score in the match?

8) Which two Australians were run out in the match?

9) Kevin Pietersen made his test debut, scoring how many runs in his first innings?

10) Glenn McGrath took his 500th test match wicket by dismissing who in the first innings?

Individual Performances – *Answers on page 28*

1) Who took the first 5 wicket haul in the series?

2) Who took the first 10 wicket haul in the series?

3) How many wickets did Shane Warne take in the series?

4) Which bowler conceded the most runs in the series?

5) Jason Gillespie played in three matches, conceding 300 runs in taking how many wickets?

6) Ashley Giles bowled 160 overs in the series, taking how many wickets?

7) Ian Bell scored 124 runs at Old Trafford (59 and 65), but how many runs did he score in the rest of the series?

8) Who was the only player to register 2 centuries in the series?

9) Who was man of the series?

Second Test – *Answers on page 30*

1) Which ground was the match played at?

2) Name the one change made by Australia

Australia	England
Justin Langer	Marcus Trescothick
Matthew Hayden	Andrew Strauss
Ricky Ponting	Michael Vaughan
Damien Martyn	Ian Bell
Michael Clarke	Kevin Pietersen
Simon Katich	Andrew Flintoff
Adam Gilchrist	Geraint Jones
Shane Warne	Ashley Giles
Brett Lee	Matthew Hoggard
Jason Gillespie	Stephen Harmison
?	Simon Jones

3) What was the result?

4) Who won the man of the match award?

5) England scored 407 runs in the first innings, how many overs did they bat for?

6) Who top scored for England in that innings?

7) Shane Warne was dismissed by Andrew Flintoff in the second innings, by what method?

8) How many runs did Brett Lee and Michael Kasprowicz add for the last wicket in the second innings at Edgbaston?

9) Which Australian was run out in this match?

Series Records – *Answers on page 32*

1) What was the highest partnership for both sides in the series?

2) What was the highest total for each team in the series?

3) What was the lowest score both teams were bowled out for in the series?

4) Who recorded the best match bowling figures for both sides?

5) Who scored the highest individual score?

6) Who had the best bowling figures in an innings for both sides?

Third Test – *Answers on page 34*

1) Which ground was the match played at?

2) Name the one change made by Australia

Australia	England
Justin Langer	Marcus Trescothick
Matthew Hayden	Andrew Strauss
Ricky Ponting	Michael Vaughan
Damien Martyn	Ian Bell
Michael Clarke	Kevin Pietersen
Simon Katich	Andrew Flintoff
Adam Gilchrist	Geraint Jones
Shane Warne	Ashley Giles
Brett Lee	Matthew Hoggard
Jason Gillespie	Stephen Harmison
?	Simon Jones

3) What was the result?

4) Who won the man of the match award?

5) Who hit the first century of the series in this game?

6) Simon Katich took his only wicket in the series in this match, who was it?
7) Geraint Jones hit a cameo of 27 runs in the second innings, off how many balls?

8) Simon Jones recorded his best career bowling performance in the first innings by taking how many wickets?

9) Who did Shane Warne dismiss to claim his 600th test wicket in this match?

Commentary – *Answers on page 36*

Can you name the commentators who delivered these lines?

1) "Steven Harmison, with a slower ball, one of the great balls. Given the moment, given the batsman, and given the match, that is a staggering gamble that's played off."

2) "Jones, Bowden. Kasprowicz the man to go. And Harmison has done it. Despair on the faces of the batsmen, and joy for every English player on the field."

3) "Bowled him! How about that! Absolutely brilliant from Shane Warne"

4) "What a performance from these two men, England have regained the ashes."

5) "That is very good, swing works the oracle again. Quite brilliant from Simon Jones."

6) "Beauty, yes, magnificent cricket from this man, really, really he's set the place alight"

7) "Oh what a catch! What a catch from Andrew Strauss, full length diving away to his left, and he's plucked one out of the air to get rid of Adam Gilchrist"

8) Out! Woah, no ball, bad luck! Oh bad luck you Aussies!

Fourth Test – *Answers on page 38*

1) Which ground was the match played at?

2) Name the two changes made by Australia

Australia	England
Justin Langer	Marcus Trescothick
Matthew Hayden	Andrew Strauss
Ricky Ponting	Michael Vaughan
Damien Martyn	Ian Bell
Michael Clarke	Kevin Pietersen
Simon Katich	Andrew Flintoff
Adam Gilchrist	Geraint Jones
Shane Warne	Ashley Giles
Brett Lee	Matthew Hoggard
?	Stephen Harmison
?	Simon Jones

3) What was the result?

4) Who won the man of the match award?

5) Which England player never represented his country again after this match?

6) What was the name of the substitute fielder who ran out Ricky Ponting in second innings?

7) Ricky Ponting took his only wicket in the series in this match, who was it?

8) Andrew Strauss took a spectacular diving catch to dismiss which batsman in the first innings?

9) Who top scored in the match?

Catches – *Answers on page 40*

1) Other than wicketkeepers, who took the most catches in the series?

2) Which two substitute fielders took catches during the series?

3) How many Catches did Kevin Pietersen drop during the series?

4) Geraint Jones took a reflex catch after the ball hit Andrew Strauss to dismiss which batsman in the second innings at Old Trafford?

5) Andrew Strauss produced perhaps the best catch of the series by diving horizontally to dismiss which batsman at Trent Bridge?

6) Who took the final catch at Edgbaston?

7) Shane Warne caught and bowled which England batsman during the second innings at the Oval?

8) Marcus Trescothick produced a brilliant diving catch to remove which batsman during the second innings at Edgbaston?

Fifth Test – *Answers on page 42*

1) Which ground was the match played at?

2) Name the change made by both side

Australia	England
Justin Langer	Marcus Trescothick
Matthew Hayden	Andrew Strauss
Ricky Ponting	Michael Vaughan
Damien Martyn	Ian Bell
Michael Clarke	Kevin Pietersen
Simon Katich	Andrew Flintoff
Adam Gilchrist	?
Shane Warne	Geraint Jones
Brett Lee	Ashley Giles
?	Matthew Hoggard
Shaun Tait	Stephen Harmison

3) What was the result?

4) Who won the man of the match award?

5) How many runs did Kevin Pietersen score during his second innings at the Oval?

6) Shane Warne dropped Kevin Pietersen during the second innings at the Oval off whose bowling?

7) Which two Australians scored their first hundreds of the series in this match?

8) Glenn McGrath had a chance to claim a hat-trick in the second innings having dismissed which two batsman in consecutive balls?

9) Who bowled the last ball of the series?

Extras – *Answers on page 44*

1) Name the four players who bowled in the series, but failed to take a wicket

2) Who hit the most 6's in the series?

3) Between the fourth and fifth tests, Australia played a two day game against Essex, which future England player scored a double century in the match?

4) Which four players were run out in the series?

5) Which company sponsored the series?

6) In which two innings were Australia not bowled out?

7) How many wickets did Australia lose in the series?

8) How many wickets did England lose in the series?

The 2006/7 Series – *Answers on page 46*

1) Can you name the two changes each side made from the final test of 2005 to the first test of the 2006/7 Ashes?

Australia	**England**
Justin Langer	Andrew Strauss
Matthew Hayden	?
Ricky Ponting	Ian Bell
Damien Martyn	Paul Collingwood
?	Kevin Pietersen
Michael Clarke	Andrew Flintoff
Adam Gilchrist	Geraint Jones
Shane Warne	Ashley Giles
Brett Lee	Matthew Hoggard
?	Stephen Harmison
Glenn McGrath	?

2) The first ball of the series was notable for what reason?

3) Who captained England in the series?

4) What was the final score in the series?

5) Who top scored for Australia in the series?

6) Who top scored for England in the series?

7) Who won the player of the series award?

8) Four Australian players from the 2005 series retired from test cricket during, or after the 2006/7 series, who were they?

Answers

Before The Series

1) What was the score in the previous ashes series in Australia in 2002/3?
   Australia won 4-1

2) What was the winning margin in the T20 international game played between the two sides?
   England won by 100 runs

3) In the T20 game, at one stage Australia lost 7 wickets for 8 runs, which two England bowlers took those 7 wickets?
   Darren Gough and Jon Lewis

4) Which other national side competed with England and Australia in the tri-nations one day competition?
   Bangladesh

5) What was the result in the final of the 50 over tri-nations competition?
   England tied with Australia

6) In the eighth match of the tri-nations series, Matthew Hayden was enraged after being hit by a throw from which England bowler?
Simon Jones

7) Following the tri-nations final, England and Australia played a further three match one day series, what was the result?
2-1 Australia

8) Which future Ashes winning fast bowler made his England debut in the tri-nations tournament?
Chris Tremlett

9) Which young Australian all-rounder was apparently scared by a ghost whilst staying at Lumley Castle before the one day international at Durham?
Shane Watson

10) Ashley Giles missed the two match test series against Bangladesh, which spinner replaced him in the side?
Gareth Batty

11) Which player made his 100th, and final, test appearance for England in that series?
Graeme Thorpe

First Test

1) Which ground was the match played at?
   Lords

2) Name the two line-ups

Australia	England
Justin Langer	Marcus Trescothick
Matthew Hayden	Andrew Strauss
Ricky Ponting	Michael Vaughan
Damien Martyn	Ian Bell
Michael Clarke	Kevin Pietersen
Simon Katich	Andrew Flintoff
Adam Gilchrist	Geraint Jones
Shane Warne	Ashley Giles
Brett Lee	Matthew Hoggard
Jason Gillespie	Stephen Harmison
Glenn McGrath	Simon Jones

3) What was the result?
   Australia Won (by 239 runs)

4) Who won the man of the match award?
   Glenn Mcgrath

5) Who bowled the first ball of the series?
   Steve Harmison

6) Who took the first wicket in the series?
   Matthew Hoggard (by bowling Matthew Hayden)

7) Which player had the highest individual score in the match?
   Michael Clarke (91 in the second innings)

8) Which two Australians were run out in the match?
   Justin Langer (by Kevin Pietersen second Innings)
   Brett Lee (by Ashley Giles second Innings)

9) Kevin Pietersen made his test debut, scoring how many runs in his first innings?
   57 (off 89 balls)

10) Glenn McGrath took his 500th test match wicket by dismissing who in the first innings?
    Marcus Trescothick

Individual Performances

1) Who took the first 5 wicket haul in the series?
Steve Harmison (At Lords first Innings)

2) Who took the first 10 wicket haul in the series?
Shane Warne (At Edgbaston)

3) How many wickets did Shane Warne take in the series?
40

4) Which bowler conceded the most runs in the series?
Brett Lee – 822

5) Jason Gillespie played in three matches, conceding 300 runs in taking how many wickets?
3

6) Ashley Giles bowled 160 overs in the series, taking how many wickets?
10

7) Ian Bell scored 124 runs at Old Trafford (59 and 65), but how many runs did he score in the rest of the series?
47 (6,8,6,21,3,3,0,0)

8) Who was the only player to register 2 centuries in the series?
Andrew Strauss (106 Old Trafford second innings and 129 The Oval first innings)

9) Who was man of the series?
Andrew Flintoff

Second Test

1) Which ground was the match played at?
   Edgbaston

2) Name the one change made by Australia

Australia	**England**
Justin Langer	Marcus Trescothick
Matthew Hayden	Andrew Strauss
Ricky Ponting	Michael Vaughan
Damien Martyn	Ian Bell
Michael Clarke	Kevin Pietersen
Simon Katich	Andrew Flintoff
Adam Gilchrist	Geraint Jones
Shane Warne	Ashley Giles
Brett Lee	Matthew Hoggard
Jason Gillespie	Stephen Harmison
Michael Kasprowicz (for Glenn McGrath)	Simon Jones

3) What was the result?
   England Won (by 2 runs)

4) Who won the man of the match award?
   Andrew Flintoff

5) England scored 407 runs in the first innings, how many overs did they bat for?
   79.2

6) Who top scored for England in that innings?
   Trescothick (90 off 102 balls)

7) Shane Warne was dismissed by Andrew Flintoff in the second innings, by what method?
   Hit Wicket

8) How many runs did Brett Lee and Michael Kasprowicz add for the last wicket in the second innings at Edgbaston?
   59

9) Which Australian was run out in this match?
   Damien Martyn (by Michael Vaughan first Innings)

Series Records

1) What was the highest partnership for both sides in the series?
   Australia - Justin Langer & Matthew Hayden (185 first wicket The Oval first innings)
   England - Andrew Flintoff & Geraint Jones (177 6th wicket Trent Bridge first innings)

2) What was the highest total for each team in the series?
   England 477 (Trent Bridge first innings)
   Australia 387 (Trent Bridge second innings)

3) What was the lowest score both teams were bowled out for in the series?
   Australia 190 (Lords first innings)
   England 155 (Lords first innings)

4) Who recorded the best match bowling figures for both sides?
   Australia - Shane Warne (The Oval) 76-8-246-12 (37.3-5-122-6 and 38.3-3-124-6)
   England - Steve Harmison (Lords) 39-6-97-8 2.48 (11.2-0-43-5 and 27.4-6-54-3)

5) Who scored the highest individual score?
   Michael Vaughan 166 (Old Trafford first innings)
   Ricky Ponting 156 (Old Trafford second Innings)

6) Who had the best bowling figures in an innings for both sides?
   Warne 23.1-7-46-6 (Edgbaston second innings)
   S Jones 17.5-6-53-6 (Old Trafford first innings)

Third Test

1) Which ground was the match played at?
   Old Trafford

2) Name the one change made by Australia

Australia	**England**
Justin Langer	Marcus Trescothick
Matthew Hayden	Andrew Strauss
Ricky Ponting	Michael Vaughan
Damien Martyn	Ian Bell
Michael Clarke	Kevin Pietersen
Simon Katich	Andrew Flintoff
Adam Gilchrist	Geraint Jones
Shane Warne	Ashley Giles
Brett Lee	Matthew Hoggard
Jason Gillespie	Stephen Harmison
Glenn McGrath (for Michael Kasprowicz)	Simon Jones

3) What was the result?
   Draw

4) Who won the man of the match award?
   Ricky Ponting

5) Who hit the first century of the series in this game?
   Michael Vaughan (first innings)

6) Simon Katich took his only wicket in the series in this match, who was it?
   Michael Vaughan (first Innings)

7) Geraint Jones hit a cameo of 27 runs in the second innings, off how many balls?
   12

8) Simon Jones recorded his best career bowling performance in the first innings by taking how many wickets?
   6 (for 53 runs)

9) Who did Shane Warne dismiss to claim his 600th test wicket in this match?
   Marcus Trescothick

Commentary

Can you name the commentators who delivered these lines?

1) "Steven Harmison, with a slower ball, one of the great balls. Given the moment, given the batsman, and given the match, that is a staggering gamble that's played off."
Mark Nicholas - Harmison bowls Clarke at Edgbaston

2) "Jones, Bowden. Kasprowicz the man to go. And Harmison has done it. Despair on the faces of the batsmen, and joy for every English player on the field."
Richie Benaud - The final ball at Edgbaston

3) "Bowled him! How about that! Absolutely brilliant from Shane Warne"
Michael Slater - Warne bowling Strauss at Edgbaston

4) "What a performance from these two men, England have regained the ashes."
Michael Atherton - as the umpires remove the bails at the end of the Oval test

5) "That is very good, swing works the oracle again. Quite brilliant from Simon Jones."
Mark Nicholas – Simon Jones bowls Clarke at Old Trafford

6) "Beauty, yes, magnificent cricket from this man, really, really he's set the place alight"
Mark Nicholas – Flintoff removes Ponting at Trent Bridge

7) "Oh what a catch! What a catch from Andrew Strauss, full length diving away to his left, and he's plucked one out of the air to get rid of Adam Gilchrist"
Michael Atherton – Strauss Catches Gilchrist at Trent Bridge

8) "Out! Woah, no ball, bad luck! Oh bad luck you Aussies!"
Geoffrey Boycott – Vaughan reprieved after being bowled by a McGrath no ball

Fourth Test

1) Which ground was the match played at?
   Trent Bridge

2) Name the two changes made by Australia

Australia	England
Justin Langer	Marcus Trescothick
Matthew Hayden	Andrew Strauss
Ricky Ponting	Michael Vaughan
Damien Martyn	Ian Bell
Michael Clarke	Kevin Pietersen
Simon Katich	Andrew Flintoff
Adam Gilchrist	Geraint Jones
Shane Warne	Ashley Giles
Brett Lee	Matthew Hoggard
Michael Kasprowicz (for Jason Gillespie)	Stephen Harmison
Shaun Tait (for Glenn McGrath)	Simon Jones

3) What was the result?
   England won (by 3 wickets)

4) Who won the man of the match award?
   Andrew Flintoff

5) Which England player never represented his country again after this match?
   Simon Jones

6) What was the name of the substitute fielder who ran out Ricky Ponting in second innings?
   Gary Pratt

7) Ricky Ponting took his only wicket in the series in this match, who was it?
   Michael Vaughan (Trent Bridge first Innings)

8) Andrew Strauss took a spectacular diving catch to dismiss which batsman in the first innings?
   Adam Gilchrist (off the bowling of Andrew Flintoff)

9) Who top scored in the match?
   Andrew Flintoff (102 of 132 balls, first innings)

Catches

1) Other than wicketkeepers, who took the most catches in the series?
Matthew Hayden - 10

2) Which two substitute fielders took catches during the series?
James Hildreth (Ricky Ponting second Innings at Lords)
Brad Hodge (Kevin Pietersen first Innings at Old Trafford and Michael Vaughan second innings at Old Trafford)

3) How many Catches did Kevin Pietersen drop during the series?
6

4) Geraint Jones took a reflex catch after the ball hit Andrew Strauss to dismiss which batsman in the second innings at Old Trafford?
Shane Warne

5) Andrew Strauss produced perhaps the best catch of the series by diving horizontally to dismiss which batsman at Trent Bridge?
Adam Gilchrist

6) Who took the final catch at Edgbaston?
Geraint Jones

7) Shane Warne caught and bowled which England batsman during the second innings at the Oval?
Andrew Flintoff

8) Marcus Trescothick produced a brilliant diving catch to remove which batsman during the second innings at Edgbaston?
Matthew Hayden

Fifth Test

1) Which ground was the match played at?
   The Oval

2) Name the change made by both sides

Australia	**England**
Justin Langer	Marcus Trescothick
Matthew Hayden	Andrew Strauss
Ricky Ponting	Michael Vaughan
Damien Martyn	Ian Bell
Michael Clarke	Kevin Pietersen
Simon Katich	Andrew Flintoff
Adam Gilchrist	Geraint Jones
Shane Warne	Ashley Giles
Brett Lee	Matthew Hoggard
Glenn McGrath (for Michael Kasprowicz)	Stephen Harmison
Shaun Tait	Simon Jones

3) What was the result?
   Draw

4) Who won the man of the match award?
   Kevin Pietersen

5) How many runs did Kevin Pietersen score during his second innings at the Oval?
158

6) Shane Warne dropped Kevin Pietersen during the second innings at the Oval off whose bowling?
Brett Lee

7) Which two Australians scored their first hundreds of the series in this match?
Justin Langer (105) and Matthew Hayden (138)

8) Glenn McGrath had a chance to claim a hat-trick in the second innings having dismissed which two batsman in consecutive balls?
Michael Vaughan and Ian Bell

9) Who bowled the last ball of the series?
Steve Harmison

Extras

1) Name the four players who bowled in the series, but failed to take a wicket
   Clarke, Collingwood, Bell, Vaughan

2) Who hit the most 6's in the series?
   Kevin Pietersen - 14

3) Between the fourth and fifth tests, Australia played a two day game against Essex, which future England player scored a double century in the match?
   Alastair Cook

4) Which four players were run out in the series?
   Justin Langer (by Kevin Pietersen second Innings Lords)
   Brett Lee (by Ashley Giles second Innings at Lords)
   Damien Martyn (by Michael Vaughan first Innings Edgbaston)
   Ricky Ponting (by Gary Pratt second Innings Trent Bridge)

5) Which company sponsored the series?
   Npower

6) In which two innings were Australia not bowled out?
   Second innings at Old Trafford and second innings at The Oval

7) How many wickets did Australia lose in the series?
   89

8) How many wickets did England lose in the series?
   93

The 2006/7 Series

1) Can you name the two changes each side made from the final test of 2005 to the first test of the 2006/7 Ashes?

   Australia   **England**
   Justin Langer   Andrew Strauss
   Matthew Hayden   **Alastair Cook**
   Ricky Ponting   Ian Bell
   Damien Martyn   Paul Collingwood
   Michael Hussey   Kevin Pietersen
   Michael Clarke   Andrew Flintoff
   Adam Gilchrist   Geraint Jones
   Shane Warne   Ashley Giles
   Brett Lee   Matthew Hoggard
   Stuart Clark   Stephen Harmison
   Glenn McGrath   **James Anderson**

2) The first ball of the series was notable for what reason?
   Steve Harmison bowled a wide which went to second slip

3) Who captained England in the series?
   Andrew Flintoff

4) What was the final score in the series?
   5-0 Australia

5) Who top scored for Australia in the series?
   Ricky Ponting

6) Who top scored for England in the series?
   Kevin Pietersen

7) Who won the player of the series award?
   Ricky Ponting

8) Four Australian players from the 2005 series retired from test cricket during, or after the 2006/7 series, who were they?
   Damien Martyn, Justin Langer, Glenn McGrath and Shane Warne

Printed in Great Britain
by Amazon